ISBN: 9781314294910

Published by:
HardPress Publishing
8345 NW 66TH ST #2561
MIAMI FL 33166-2626

Email: info@hardpress.net
Web: http://www.hardpress.net

The
OSEBERG SHIP

by

ANTON WILHELM BRÖGGER

Professor of Archæology in the
University of Christiania

■

Price Fifty Cents

Reprinted from
The American-Scandinavian Review
July 1921

The Oseberg Ship

By Anton Wilhelm Brögger

The ships of the Viking Age discovered in Norway count among the few national productions of antiquity that have attained world wide celebrity. And justly so, for they not only give remarkable evidence of a unique heathen burial custom, but they also bear witness to a very high culture which cannot fail to be of interest to the world outside. The Oseberg discoveries, the most remarkable and abundant antiquarian find in Norway, contain a profusion of art, a wealth of objects and phenomena, coming from a people who just at that time, the ninth century, began to come into contact with one-half of Europe. It was a great period and it has given us great monuments. We have long been acquainted with its literature. Such a superb production as Egil Skallagrimson's *Sonartorrek,* which is one hundred years later than the Oseberg material, is a worthy companion to it.

The Oseberg ship was dug out of the earth and caused the greatest astonishment even among Norwegians. Who could know that on that spot, an out of the way barrow on the farm of Oseberg in the parish of Slagen, a little to the north of Tönsberg, there would be excavated the finest and most abundant antiquarian discoveries of Norway? It was in the summer of the year 1903 that a farmer at Oseberg began to dig the barrow. He struck some woodwork and stopped digging. A journey to Christiania brought him in touch with Professor G. Gustafson, at that time director of the University Collection of Antiquities, to whom he made known his discovery. Gustafson at once went to the spot, and made a small trial excavation, which after a day or so convinced him that the barrow contained a Viking ship, as large as the Gokstad ship excavated near Sandefjord in 1880. On that hypothesis he was able to plan his excavations.

THE SHIP AS IT LAY IN THE BARROW AFTER THE EXCAVATIONS WERE COMPLETED

which took place throughout the summer of 1904, and were not concluded until late in the autumn. The task was long and difficult, but the result was a complete romance. That such an achievement was made, and that the Oseberg discoveries obtained so great historical importance are very largely due to the enormous care and energy displayed by Professor Gustafson. He did not live to see the completion of the work of preparing the material discovered, dying in the midst of his labors in April, 1915.

The barrow in which the discovery was made was situated close to an ancient river bed, five kilometers from the sea. During the Viking Age the river was navigable for a vessel of the size of the Oseberg ship.) The barrow was at one time one of the largest in Norway, but in the course of centuries had been completely destroyed. It was built of huge masses of peat, and formed a completely airtight covering over the whole of the interior, and in conjunction with the foundation of clay in which all the objects lay, it resulted in the excellent state of preservation which characterizes the material excavated. All the wooden objects were preserved, although broken by mechanical means, through the great pressure of the masses of earth above.

The ship lay in the barrow pointing north to south, with the prow toward the south. Behind the mast there was a sepulchral chamber of timber in which lay the dead. Stones were thrown over the whole of the ship, and above them the barrow was erected. At the very commencement of the excavations, those engaged found proofs that the barrow had been broken into in ancient times, and the course of the thieves could be distinctly traced. From the southern side of the mound they penetrated to the middle by means of an open passage some three or four meters in breadth, with the sole object of reaching the sepulchral chamber. It was evident that they had succeeded in doing so, for the chamber bore very distinct traces of their work. They chopped out a large opening in the tent-shaped roof, and took

DETAIL OF A POST ORNAMENTED WITH ANIMAL HEADS

away a considerable quantity of the valuables which must undoubtedly have been in the chamber. This compartment contained the bodies of two women, the Oseberg Queen and her bond-woman. We can see how the robbers desecrated the corpses by chopping off arms and hands which presumably bore gold rings. Traces of the robbers were found all over the passages along which they had forced an entrance. Here and there lay broken remains of objects which had lain in the sepulchral chamber.

From the level of the thieves' entrance an investigation was by degrees made of the sepulchral chamber. There had lain the two dead women, presumably each in a separate bed, surrounded by coverlets, pillows, and clothes. One of the women, perhaps the Queen herself, must have been about thirty years of age, the other about fifty. The sepulchral chamber in the ship was made their resting place,

THE BIG OAK CHEST

and with them were placed a number of articles of a more personal character. We must content ourselves by mentioning the most important. There was a beautiful oak chest containing both fruit and grain, viz., wild apples (crab-apples) and wheat. Wild apples were found in other parts of the ship, and in all we have now about fifty of them. We may here mention that the vegetable remains from the Oseberg ship are in such considerable quantities, that they prove with certainty that, assuming the year to have been a normal one from the point of view of vegetation, the burial of the Oseberg Queen must have taken place at the end of August or during the first week of September.

Two other chests were found in the chamber, both of oak. One of them was quite entire, and contained two iron lamps with long rods, a wooden box for cotton, an awl, a spindle, iron scissors, horseshoe nails, etc. In general, the sepulchral chamber contained a collection of domestic implements. We may mention a winder for yarn, and also two looms, both of very important and interesting types. In this connection we may also mention the most remarkable contents of the sepulchral chamber, the numerous remnants of woven picture tapestries which lay there. At the present time a scientific assistant to the Editorial Committee is working at this material, and it may be said, inter alia, that these tapestries must to a large extent have been made in Norway.

In another part of the sepulchral chamber was found a collection of buckets and pails. Two of these belong to the most beautiful objects in the entire collection, one having four handles and a wealth of brass fittings, the unique form of which has given rise to the incorrect name "Buddha" pail, whereas the workmanship is Western and most probably English, belonging to the early Viking period.

It should also be mentioned that the sepulchral chamber once contained two beds, a large quantity of rope for

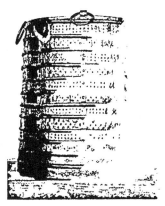

LARGE PAIL WITH BRASS MOUNTINGS

tents and sails, a considerable quantity of down and feathers for pillows and coverlets, a number of unique and beautifully carved wooden poles representing the heads of animals, and further a quantity of large and small objects of various kinds.

When the investigation of the sepulchral chamber was completed, it was possible to proceed with the stern of the ship. The space was small, but nevertheless it contained a number of the objects belonging to a tidy and well-appointed kitchen, such as an iron pot with a three-legged stand, a chain for a hanging pot, a number of small dishes and troughs of wood, frying pans, kit-boxes, knives, a hand-mill for corn, a kitchen stool with four legs, and a great many other articles. In the stern there also lay a small axe. It was placed between two oak planks and was wonderfully well preserved.

That which was found in the sepulchral chamber and in the stern, however, was nothing in comparison with that found in the fore part of the ship. It is only possible to enumerate here the most important of the objects discovered. As regards ships' equipment here were found a number of oars, a gangway plank, two water barrels, booms and gaffs for spreading sails, bailing scoops, anchors and anchor stocks, in addition to a number of indeterminate objects which undoubtedly belong to the equipment of a ship. Among the burial equipment may be mentioned, first and foremost, the beautiful four-wheeled wagon, which is one of the most remarkable objects in the Ose-

The So-Called Buddha Pail

berg collection. As will be seen, it was intended to be drawn by two horses, and has a most curious construction, there being a loose wagon body made of oak. On the sides of the latter we find some very interesting and remarkable carvings in the oak. As regards other vehicles, there were four sledges, three of which are very beautiful and luxurious, with richly carved bodies. These, too, were intended for two horses. There were also discovered three beds, the framework for two tents, one framework for a very large tent, a chair,

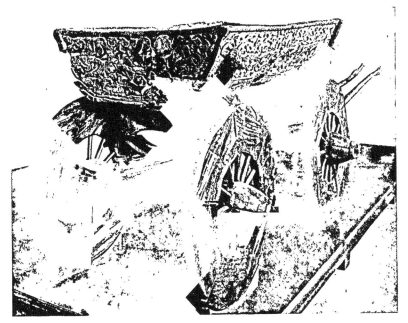

THE OSEBERG WAGON

a trough containing rye flour, several wooden dishes, a box or basket made of bast, two buckets, one of which contained combs, balls of thread, wax, buckles, mountings, and in addition seeds of the woad plant which was used for dyeing, and also flax seeds and wild apples. There were further a litter or stretcher, a number of spades, three pairs of shoes, a ribbon loom, a beautifully carved pole representing an animal's head, three sledge poles, harness for horses and chains for dogs. Finally, in addition to all the above, there were the remains of fifteen horses, four dogs and an ox. It was certainly not a cheap funeral!

In the fore part of the vessel oars had been stuck out through openings in the ship's side ready for the voyage. In other words, it was intended that the Queen should be able to use the ship just as she had done during her lifetime.

It was not until the end of September, 1904, that all the different objects had been excavated, and for the first time since its burial the Oseberg ship lay uncovered. It was not a pleasing sight, twisted as it was by the masses of earth, the bottom of the ship pushed up by the underlying clay, broken, warped, all the boards crushed and loosened, the ribs sundered and partly destroyed. The ship required to

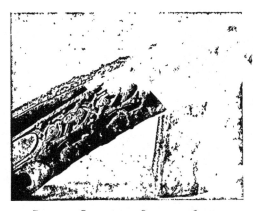

DETAILS OF CARVING FROM ONE OF THE SLEDGES

be taken out as quickly as possible, but that could of course not be done except piece by piece. An expert ships' engineer supervised the work, which proceeded until the Oseberg ship, in about 2,000 pieces, reached Christiania at the end of December, 1904. There it was at first stored, and then, after a lengthy restoration, was re-erected on the spot where it stands today.

The Oseberg ship itself is a large, open boat, twenty meters long on her keel, and about twenty-four meters from stem to stern. The breadth is very great, being more than five meters, and the vessel is quite flat-bottomed, being intended to sail in very shallow water. The height above the water-line is quite inappreciable. She has seventeen ribs and holds (or intermediate spaces), all the important parts being made of oak, and there are fifteen holes for oars on each side, so that thirty men were required to row the ship. But in addition she has

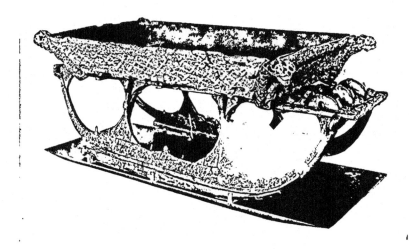

ONE OF THE RICHLY ORNAMENTED SLEDGES

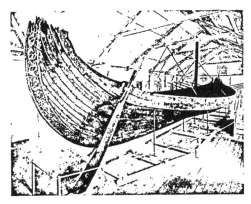

a pine-mast for a sail. There was a deck or flooring. The ship was steered by means of a rudder placed on the starboard side aft. Thus the Oseberg ship was not a sea-going boat like the Gokstad ship, so that it would not be possible to sail to America in the Oseberg ship, as Magnus Andersen did in a replica of the Gokstad ship in 1893, although the two vessels are almost of the same size. But the reason is that the purpose of the two vessels was different. One was a sea-going ship, the other a pleasure boat. The Oseberg ship was the Queen's yacht for summer cruises along the Norwegian coast within the sheltered waters inside the skerries. The stem and stern of the ship are richly decorated, with beautiful carvings of animals. This is the first monumental work of Norwegian art. The great profusion of art in the Oseberg discoveries represents new acquisitions for the history of Norwegian culture and is of the utmost importance. It is Norwegian in spirit and in execution. The subjects are, of course, the result of influences from various parts of Europe, but in scarcely any country of Europe can we find at that time,—the decades succeeding the death of Charlemagne,—such a rich, independent, and fruitful art as that which the Oseberg discoveries have reveled to us in Norway.

There is one very natural question which every one will ask when reading of the Oseberg Queen and her treasures. Who was she? The present author, in a work published in 1915, endeavored to prove that we can connect this remarkable group of discoveries of ships with a special Norwegian princely family, that which commenced the conquest of Norway from Vestfold. By means of detailed investigations, which space does not permit us to refer to here, the author has tried to show that the Oseberg Queen must be a certain Queen Asa, who was the mother of King Halfdan the Black, and also the grandmother of King Harald the Fair-haired. She was married to King Godröd in Vestfold, but against her will. The year after Halfdan was born she caused her husband to be killed in revenge for his having taken away and killed her father and brother. It is on account of this fearful deed that her name is preserved in our history. But she was a remarkable woman, loved and feared. She brought up her son Halfdan the Black, and gave him lofty ideals regarding his vocation. Her figure stands out in history as fully worthy of the picture we obtain of her by means of the Oseberg discoveries.

CARVED ANIMAL HEADS

ImTheStory.com

Personalized Classic Books in many genre's

Unique gift for kids, partners, friends, colleagues

Customize:

- Character Names
- Upload your own front/back cover images (optional)
- Inscribe a personal message/dedication on the
  inside page (optional)

Customize many titles Including
- Alice in Wonderland
- Romeo and Juliet
- The Wizard of Oz
- A Christmas Carol
- Dracula
- Dr. Jekyll & Mr. Hyde
- And more...

CPSIA information can be obtained
at www.ICGtesting.com
Printed in the USA
LVOW04s1229160116

470068LV00041B/719/P